Down-Home Philosophy and Advice from Country's Biggest Stars

Bruce Nash and Allan Zullo
Compiled by Liz Johnson

Andrews and McMeel
A Universal Press Syndicate Company
Kansas City

Library of Congress Cataloging-in-Publication Data

Talkin' country : down-home philosophy and advice from country's biggest stars / [concept by] Bruce Nash and Allan Zullo ; compiled by Liz Johnson.

    p. cm.
  ISBN 0-8362-8067-9 : $6.95
  1. Conduct of life. 2. Country musicians—Quotations. I. Nash, Bruce M.
II. Zullo, Allan. III. Johnson, Liz. IV. Title: Talking country.
BJ1611.2.T34   1994
818'.5402080927816—dc20   94-20930
                                              CIP

Book design and illustrations by Barrie Maguire

DEDICATION

To Dennis Bogorad, whose deeds speak volumes about his
commitment, concern, and compassion.

—BRUCE NASH

To Lowell and Priscilla Flowers, what country folks
are meant to be.

—ALLAN ZULLO

Talkin' Country

From Roy Acuff to Tammy Wynette, the stars of country music have a lot to say even when they're not in front of a microphone singing their hearts out.

We can learn a thing or two from the philosophy, insights, and reflections of our favorite country stars who have written and recorded their universally-appealing songs.

Sometimes they offer simple advice, such as Patsy Cline's suggestion to women: "Keep your chin up and your skirt down." Other times, their words of wisdom have been passed down through generations, such as the advice given to Billy Ray Cyrus by his father: "There're only two things in the middle of the road—yellow lines and dead possums."

In *Talkin' Country,* you will discover the private feelings, dreams, aspirations, and philosophies of top country singers. This unique book reveals the down-home views on topics that country stars sing about most—including love, divorce, family, fame, and heartache.

From legends such as Chet Atkins and Loretta Lynn to today's hot performers, including Garth Brooks and Wynonna, country stars offer you their thoughts—all uttered in their own inimitable style.

But enough talking about the book. It's time to start . . .

Talkin' Country!

ACCEPTANCE

Nobody is going to like you all of the time. I'm sure there are people who would like to slap my hair off.
—Dolly Parton

ACCOMPLISHMENTS

Feeling good comes from making other people feel good. That's the reward that comes from being an entertainer.
—Mel McDaniel

Some of the greatest accomplishments in the world have been performed by old men. So you're never washed up. You can always accomplish something. But you'll never do it if you retire and just sit.

—Tex Ritter

AGE

If I'd known I was gonna live this long, I'd have taken better care of myself.
—Waylon Jennings

Don't let your age have anything to do with your lifestyle. I don't look my age, so why should I act it?
—Dottie West

Just because you're twice as old as someone doesn't mean you're twice as wise. But it does mean you've survived twice as long.
—Hal Ketchum

ALTRUISM

I know I can't change the world, but I know I can try.
—Reba McEntire

In one aspect, being called a "hunk" is probably as offensive as it is for a blonde actress being called a dumb airhead.
—Travis Tritt

APPEARANCE

Wouldn't it be great to be a woman and be just like Willie Nelson? I've often thought, "God, that would be great to be the first woman out there with wrinkles and not trying to cover it up."
—Lacy J. Dalton

It takes a lot of money to make me look this cheap.
—Dolly Parton

ATTITUDES

When you're in a sad state of mind, try the sad songs. It helps heal the pain.
—Reba McEntire

talking about the album dedicated to eight members of her performing family who were killed in a plane crash

If you've got a bad attitude, then you are going to have bad things happen to you.
—Earl Thomas Conley

Don't believe your own press, because sometimes it will knock you down.
—Chris Hillman
of the Desert Rose Band

CAREERS

There are no rules to making it in a career. I used to think there was a method to the madness. I thought if you did A, B, C, D, and E, by the time you get to F, you'd be winning awards. Then I got to F, G, and H and didn't get anything. You just have to do your best, and get on with it.

—Collin Raye

I don't think people can be happy at home unless they are happy in their career. I think you have to have a well-rounded life.

—Cheryl White
of The Whites

Every career has peaks and valleys. Once you under-stand that, you can usually make it through anything.

—Tammy Wynette

CHALLENGES

Whatever you do in life, you better have fun with it.
—David Frizzell

If you raise a 400-pound hog and you're not careful, it'll turn around and eat you.
—Conway Twitty
on letting your career consume you

Never let the mountains facing you get you down. If I take a notion to do something, you can bet I'll go all the way with it. I won't stop until I get there. I'm a mountain climber, and every morning I wake up and say, "Another new mountain and it's a little bit bigger." The bigger the hill, the better I feel.

—Loretta Lynn

CHANGE

You can't be afraid of change—I wouldn't be here today if I hadn't taken some chances and made some changes.
—Aaron Tippin

I believe in change. It's the only thing I know of that's constant. When things stop changin', they die.
—Conway Twitty

CHEATING

I'm a family person. I don't cheat on my wife. A man has to have principles. When you turn your back on your principles, you turn your back on yourself.
—David Allan Coe

My attitude toward men who mess around is simple: If you find 'em, kill 'em.
—Loretta Lynn

CONFIDENCE

Don't let other people's lack of confidence in you stop you from trying. It's always great to prove them wrong.
— *Travis Tritt*

There's one word you should never let stand in your way, and that's the word "no." You've got to be thick-skinned when you hear it, and remember that some-body out there will probably say "yes."
— Tammy Wynette

CONSCIENCE

When your intelligence don't tell you somethin' ain't right, your conscience gives you a tap on the shoulder and says, "Hold on." If it don't, you're a snake.
— *Elvis Presley*

Dig down deep in your heart and find out what's right, and that'll tell you what's wrong.
— *Waylon Jennings*

COUNTRY MUSIC

You know what you get when you play country music backwards? You get your wife back, your house back, and your car back.
—Clint Black

COWBOYS

If everybody thought more like a cowboy in this rat race society of ours, a lot of problems could be cured. People have lost their values in the '90s, and they don't appreciate the simple things.
—Toby Keith

CRITICISM

God didn't make skyscrapers or pollution or crowded streets. The deity we all believe in made mountains, streams, horses and other animals, and a lot of fish. I figure he must be a cowboy.
—Dan Seals

Never be afraid of criticism. I never had any animosity towards anybody turning me down. If it wasn't for critics, we wouldn't learn a thing.
—Doug Supernaw

DARK SIDE

I do dwell on the dark side of things. I write about things I know: depression, guilt, despair, failed relationships. Take the dark side and make it work for you.
—**Mary-Chapin Carpenter**

People always have to guard themselves against their demons. Know what they are, and how to fight them. I've got that wild streak—that black dog inside of me that wants to bite—so I watch for signs that it's starting to growl.
—*Johnny Cash*

DEATH

DISAPPOINTMENTS

Death doesn't end things. I don't think anyone ever stops, really. I think we keep on goin' till we get it right.
—Loretta Lynn

who believes she was a Native American and an Irish girl in previous lives

It's not the years that bring you down. It's the passing of the caskets.
—Jerry Lee Lewis

Career-wise, there have been many disappointments. But it's through those disappointments that you grow. As somebody said, if show business was easy, everybody would be doing it.
—Minnie Pearl

DIVORCE

You have one primary directive when you're going through a divorce—keep your children from believing it is their fault.
—Gary Morris

When it comes to talking about your divorce, I've learned the best comment is no comment. It's best to keep your private life private.
—Reba McEntire

DOGS

The late columnist Lewis Grizzard had a theory about why divorced men buy dogs. He said that it's because no matter how late you come in or what shape you're in, the dog is happy to see you. I've got to agree with that.
—Travis Tritt

DREAMS

Always have a dream that's just around the corner. I reached a point in my life where my dreams had pretty much come true, and after a while it dawned on me that I forgot to get some new dreams and set some new goals.

—Steve Earle

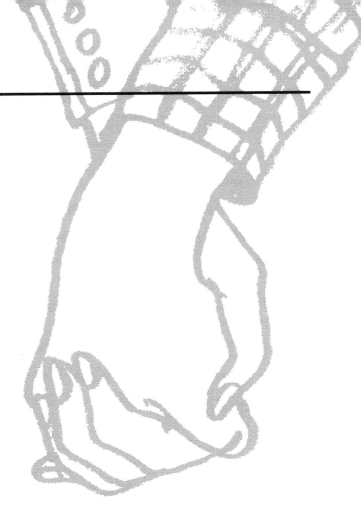

I wrote a line once that said, "Be careful what you're dreaming or soon your dreams will be dreaming you." And so, whatever you're dreaming, if it's good dreams or bad dreams, that determines what is going to happen next. Your dreams are going to come true.
—Willie Nelson

You have to have dreams and aspirations and be able to come back from a knock-down punch. That's how to keep on going through tough times.
—Bob Carpenter
of the Nitty Gritty Dirt Band

I have new dreams every day. That way some of them will come true.
—Dolly Parton

EATING

I'm a big eater. I really like to eat, so I have to watch it. But when I go back home, to Texas, I've got to have a great big chicken fried steak, mashed potatoes and gravy, biscuits—everything! You can't always deny yourself the things you want, because that's not living.
—Tanya Tucker

One of my best friends once gave me some great advice: "When in doubt, eat chocolate."
—Lacy J. Dalton

EFFORT

There ought to be an award for people who endure. The trick to life is just hanging in there.
—Howard Bellamy
of the Bellamy Brothers

You can't hit a home run every time you're up to bat, but you can sure try.
—Charley Pride

Never give just 50 percent of what you've got. It's not even that you owe that to someone else, it's that you owe it to yourself.
—Gary Morris

There's one sure way to get what you want in life, and that's to work hard for it.
—Loretta Lynn

The harder I work, the luckier I get.
—Toby Keith

Sometimes you get ahead by stupidity and ignorance, by not knowing things. You keep on plugging away because you don't know any better.
—Tammy Wynette

Envy someone and it pulls you down. Admire them and it builds you up. Which makes more sense?
—Elvis Presley

EXPERIENCE

Experience is the best teacher, and a lot of us had to learn things the hard way.
　　　　—George Jones

Experience is a hard teacher. She gives the tests first and the lessons come after.
　　　　—Patsy Cline

FAILURE

If you think about failing, you probably won't even try. That's the real failure.
　　　　—Tanya Tucker

All failure means is that you took a shot.
　　　　—John Hartford

The only time you really fail is when you fail yourself.
　　　　—Gary Morris

FAITH

You're bound to fail if you start out in a career just looking for awards and honors. You should start out because you love doing something and you do it well. That philosophy will keep you on track.
— **Doug Phelps**
of Brother Phelps

I believe in the hereafter, and that this life is the training ground for it. That's why you better live like you're in the Lord's training camp, because you are.
—Merle Haggard

If there's a decision to be made, I simply put it in God's hands, and things just begin to fall into place.
—*Barbara Mandrell*

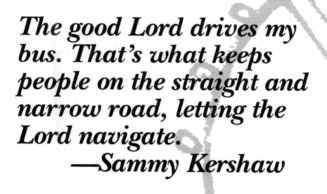

The good Lord drives my bus. That's what keeps people on the straight and narrow road, letting the Lord navigate.
　　　　　—Sammy Kershaw

I'm one of those people who believes in miracles. I just have this gut feeling that everything's gonna be all right. If you believe that way, more often than not, it really will turn out all right.
—Dolly Parton

Sometimes the Lord has to hit us with a sledgehammer to knock a little sense into our heads.
—George Jones

FAME

You're only as hot as your last hit. Fame is fleeting.
—T. Graham Brown

Ain't nowhere else in the world but the good ol' U.S.A. where you can go from driving a truck to driving a Cadillac overnight. Nowhere.
—Elvis Presley

If you seek fame, ultimately it will destroy you.
—Rosanne Cash

Never desire fame. Just the trappings.
—Kris Kristofferson

FAMILY

Above all, listen to your parents, because you only have one set. Make them proud and you will achieve your greatest wish in life.
        —Patsy Cline

The biggest mistake you can make when you're young is to lie to your folks. Always remember—you can't hide nothing from your mama.
        —Aaron Tippin

The good thing about being a middle child is that you have one sibling to look after you and one you can boss around.

—Louise Mandrell

There's no greater compliment you can give your parents than to say you want to be just like them. I have always tried to pattern myself after my father and mother. It is their image that keeps me hurrying home to be with my family.
—Barbara Mandrell

Respect people's family if you want to get along with them. You can mess with my music; you can tell me you hate it or it's not any good. You can even make fun of me. But don't make fun of my mother, my sister, or my animals. I will bomb your house.
—Wynonna

FEARS

You can't be creative when you're scared to death of failing.
—*Holly Dunn*

Fear can work for you. I'll worry myself to death over little things, but I'd rather do that than go through life carefree and put it in someone else's hands, then all of a sudden get hit with a big whammy.
—Travis Tritt

Fear can get your motor running even on a cold morning. If you fear you're losing ground at something, then let the adrenalin kick in to make you work harder.
—*Joe Sun*

FORGIVENESS

I had some bad old days. I always remember that God forgives, though, and one of the worst things you can do is not to forgive yourself.
—Johnny Cash

FUTURE

I have enough trouble trying to keep up with tomorrow without worrying about the distant future.
—Doug Supernaw

The Hopi Indians say before you do something, you should think about how it will affect the next seven generations.
—Rosanne Cash

GENIUS

I had a piano teacher when I was twelve, and she once told me, "There is no such thing as genius. All genius is, is the ability to take pain." That sounds a little strange at first, but it's true. I think if you sit there and try long enough, you could be a blathering idiot like me and finally latch onto something that's really good.
—Ray Stevens

GETTING THERE

You can't ever let up. Sometimes you have to be under the gun to really get out there and crank.
—Steve Goetzman
of Exile

People are always saying "There's a light at the end of the tunnel." I always ask, "How long's the tunnel?"
—J.P. Pennington
of Exile

Sometimes you can't take the long range focus, you just have to nibble away at it day by day.

—Howard Bellamy

of the Bellamy Brothers

If you can conceive it and you can believe it, you can achieve it.

—Naomi Judd

There have been lots of times when it's been rough. But I always knew that it would smooth out. If I didn't like the road I was walkin' on, I'd start gradin' another one.

—Dolly Parton

Part of my theory on getting to the top of a profession is that it's like mountain climbing. One way is you can climb your way to the top. The other way is that somebody can drop you off with a helicopter. The guy who climbed up there knows how to get back down, but the guy who got dropped off has to wait for another helicopter.

—Kenny Rogers

You always want to put your foot forward, to try to get someplace and not go backwards. You might think you're just plodding along, but you're still moving ahead.

—Holly Dunn

GOALS

Goals that you have feel different once you get there. Sometimes attaining them is even more rewarding than you thought, and other times you wonder why you even had that goal.
— Kathy Mattea

If you can define in life what you want to do, set your goal and don't change it.
— Patsy Cline

When you're on a team, working toward a goal, the only way you're going to make it happen is if you really live by the rule: One for all and all for one.
— Marty Roe
of Diamond Rio

Having goals is what propels you through choppy waters. You'll keep on paddling because you figure that things are smoother just around the bend. And who knows, they just might be.
—Joe Sun

You get knocked down some days. Life is not always easy; new days sometimes present new obstacles and new challenges. But I think it is important to seek our visions, and not to lose sight of our goals.
—William Lee Golden
of the Oak Ridge Boys

GUILT

A man has to know what he wants to do, and then do it and keep his mind on it, and don't let nothing else get in the way to clutter up his life.
—Hank Williams

Sometimes I feel guilty because I'm not that interesting of a person. You have to work against guilt feelings, because they'll defeat you.
—Joe Diffie

HAPPINESS

You don't always have to set the woods on fire to be happy in life. When you get grown, you learn how to live and not let things bother you. I've always been laid back, but now I'm glued back.
—Vern Gosdin

I'm never happy unless I'm walkin' on hot coals and dodging bullets.
—Garth Brooks

Always stop and remember that happiness doesn't come from having everything you want, but in understanding and accepting all, and in the prayer and belief that everything always happens for the best.
—Willie Nelson
in a letter to his children

You can't get too happy over the good things, or too sad over the bad things.
—Willie Nelson

Happiness is not at the end of life, but all along the way.
—Naomi Judd

Happiness and success not only do not run around together, it is doubtful they even know one another.
—Tom T. Hall

Happiness? I think it comes from the people you love more than the things you accomplish.
—Ronnie Milsap

HARD TIMES

Times get hard, but there are ways to get by. If you don't mind cooking and washing dishes, you can usually find a job somewhere. I'm living proof of that. Just keep on trying.

—Randy Travis

Hard times will come again. Hard times don't hide from anybody.

—John Anderson

HEALTH

One thing you simply cannot take for granted is good health. Every morning you should get up and thank God that you feel good.
—Barbara Mandrell

After surviving my heart attack, I find that even ugly people look pretty now.
—Vern Gosdin

Sometimes people need to cry as much as they need to laugh. And the end result is the same—they feel better.
—Steve Earle

HEROES

I have two heroes. God and Hank Williams. Make sure you hold up the very best as your ideals.
— George Jones

The biggest heroes to me are the people who haven't had things given to them, and who work hard every day trying to make it. I don't think you hear the working class whining as much as the people who've had everything handed over on a silver platter.
— David Allan Coe

HILLBILLIES

Don't let "name tags" bother you or make any difference in your work. People have called me "the glitterbilly kid" because of my clothes and hair. But basically I'm just a hillbilly singer in rhinestones. Cash with flash, I think somebody wrote once.
— Marty Stuart

The four things a hillbilly singer needs are a Cadillac, a Nudie cowboy suit, the right hairdo, and a pair of pointy-toed boots.
— Marty Stuart

You got to have smelled a lot of mule manure before you can sing like a hillbilly.
— Hank Williams

HONESTY

Allow people to know what you really are, not just the front they might see. I'd rather people know me, the truthful woman, than for me to be put on a pedestal where I don't belong. I'd rather they know I'm just a plain human being.
—Tammy Wynette

Shoot straight and keep things on the square. If you do that, things will work out in life.
—John Conlee

If you're honest, you can live with yourself and nobody can hurt you.
—Lane Brody

IDEAL WOMAN

If you're going to make mistakes, at least make them honest ones.
—Razzy Bailey

I'm gonna go out and find me a girl who can suck the chrome off a trailer hitch.
—Willie Nelson

IMAGE

Don't try to cultivate an image that's not you. I'm not looking to get a good guy image. I don't think good guy images are beneficial to anybody. And I'm not necessarily a good guy.
—Rodney Crowell

You have to be very careful how you draw attention to yourself. I don't understand getting attention in a negative way. I just feel that I'm too intelligent to take my clothes off to get somebody's attention.
—Charly McClain

The more people know about you, the less they want to know. Don't ever lose your mystique.
—Conway Twitty

Heart wins over looks every time. You can have the sexy image and the Bob Mackie wardrobe, but if the heart isn't there, it isn't worth anything.
—Dottie West

There's this guy I'd love to be, then there's this guy I seem to be, and I'm really somewhere in between. In deep water.
—Merle Haggard

INDIVIDUALITY

I never liked being just one of the crowd. If you want to be different, though, think up positive ways to do it. Too many times people try to get noticed the wrong way.
—Sylvia

I've always felt like a fire-ball in a freezer. But you can draw strength from being an outsider.
—Shelby Lynn

KNOWLEDGE

Always operate on the theory that everybody is 50 percent right.

—Tom T. Hall

Sometimes the road that leads to any kind of knowledge is too rocky and hard to be worth the knowledge.
—June Carter Cash

LESSONS

The most important lesson you can learn is just be yourself. When I first started out in music, I wanted to be Keith Whitley or Merle Haggard or George Strait. Then I found out I couldn't be Keith Whitley or Merle Haggard or George Strait. But I could be John Michael Montgomery.

—John Michael Montgomery

The reason you have a bad experience is to teach you not to do it again.
—Willie Nelson

There are a few lessons you can't learn too young. If you jump right into the skillet, you'll fry pretty fast.
—Conway Twitty

I think the mid-life crisis has been given a bad rap. My life has just turned upside down, but it's great. A mid-life crisis gives you so many opportunities to learn and grow.
—Rodney Crowell
after his divorce from Rosanne Cash

LIFE

Kirk Douglas gave me some advice on acting that works in a lot of life's situations. He said, "Just do your lines and don't bump into any furniture."
—Johnny Cash

As life goes on, things get harder, but more rewarding.
—Merle Haggard

Don't hurry your life.
—Mel Tillis

I'm thankful I was able to make a mark in this world. Too many people are born into this world, and live and die, and the only people who know they existed are their immediate family.
—David Allan Coe

I once saw an epitaph that read, "As you are now, I once was. As I am now, you soon shall be." That got my attention, don't you know.
—Chet Atkins

Change the things you can, accept the things you can't, and don't you ever forget that you're your best friend.
—Donna Fargo

People say life is short, and that's true. But it can be broad.
—*Johnny Cash*

Life is a little like a bottle of Jim Beam. It mellows some over the years.
—Hank Williams, Jr.

Life is about giving back to others.
—*Steve Wariner*

Live fast, love hard, and die young.
—Faron Young
. . . his country credo

Life is too short. You should live each day as if it's your last. God didn't promise us tomorrow—we have today.
—Barbara Mandrell

Life was simpler before we had forty channels and the sky was full of satellites.
—Hal Ketchum

LOVE

*You know what love is?
When you hold your little
baby in your arms for the first
time. That's it. That's love.
After that, forget it, friends.
—Loretta Lynn*

When you have real love, you don't have to work all that hard to keep it alive.
　　　—Richard Sterban
of the Oak Ridge Boys

Love is love. If it's blind, you don't know it until you're completely in the dark.
　　　—Del Woods

Real love is forgiveness of each other's faults.
　　　—Earl Thomas Conley

I think one thing I've learned is I can't give my heart again until someone gives it back.
　　　—Lorrie Morgan

LOVERS

You always need to remember to love your partner a little more than you love yourself.
　　　—Jessi Colter

Aside from being the best of lovers, you have to be the best of friends.
　　　—Lorrie Morgan

MAKING IT

It's a hard lesson, but an important one: While you are trying to make it, people will pull for you. Sometimes when you get there, not many are left patting you on the back.
—Randy Travis

Don't feel down if you don't succeed right away. I don't think overnight success is ever as rewarding as when it takes you a period of time to make it. That way you can get used to each level as you go along, and keep your priorities straight.
—Kathy Mattea

MARRIAGE

Marriage is only hard if you make it hard.
　　　　　—Duane Allen
of the Oak Ridge Boys

The way to keep a husband from wishing he was single is to give him breathing room.
　　　　　—Louise Mandrell

Nobody, man or woman, has ever wrecked a good marriage.
　　　　　—Jimmy Dean

My wife likes to cook, and I like to eat.
　　　　　—Randy Travis
on why his marriage is solid

A little bit of give and take keeps a marriage working. You have to keep thinking that there's nothing so bad that it can't get worked out.
　　　　　—Kitty Wells

The two most important things in a marriage are communication and a sense of humor.
—Martina McBride

The secret to making a marriage work is this: Don't harbor grudges, and don't pull any punches.
—Barbara Mandrell

Every material possession you acquire becomes a stick to beat you with. Live simply.
—Rosanne Cash

MEMORIES

Memories cut both ways. There's no way to forget the worst pain, but nothin' gives you the same kind of pleasure as rememberin' your greatest happiness.
—Elvis Presley

MISTAKES

The mistakes you make should be between you and the Lord.
—Clint Black

Don't apologize for every failure. I've made about every mistake a man can make, and even repeated a few of 'em.
—Johnny Paycheck

The easiest and maybe biggest mistake you can make is biting off more than you can chew.

—Earl Thomas Conley

What is a mistake but a lesson you've learned the hard way?

—Joe Sun

If you let every mistake you make trip you up, you'll be doing nothing but stumbling the rest of your life.

—David Allan Coe

Don't side-step the mistakes you've made. Don't deny 'em. Above all, don't forget 'em.

—Aaron Tippin

MONEY

I've been broke before and will be again. Heartbroke? That's serious. Lose a few bucks? That's not.
— *Willie Nelson*
after the IRS socked him
with a bill for $16.7 million

Money is like oxygen. You've got to have it to live.
—Wynonna

My mother once told me, "No wealth or position can endure, unless built upon truth and justice." Therefore, I will engage in no transaction that does not benefit all whom it attracts.
—Willie Nelson

I think when you work with people who are good in anything, it kind of ups your own level. It's like that in movies, in music, and in sports. If I play golf with somebody who's really good, I'll try harder and probably have a better game.
—George Strait

MUSIC

Success simply cannot be allowed to overshadow what it is that you've been trying to do along the way. I never want the spectacle or the success to outweigh the music.
— Garth Brooks

Politics and music mix about as well as liquor and love.
— Loretta Lynn

Even a bad night of music beats the best day you'll ever have in the heating and air-conditioning business.
— Travis Tritt

I spent the early part of my life looking at the north end of a southbound mule. It didn't take me long to figure out that a guitar was a lot lighter than a plow handle.
—Glen Campbell

There's no room for negativity anymore. Let's make sure that life is a beautiful thing for everybody. That's the way I live my life now.
—Shania Twain

PARENTHOOD

I don't think you are ever really ready to be a mother. It's not the easiest job in the world, but it's definitely the most rewarding.

—Marie Osmond

When you feel like giving up, or you're so tired you think you can't make it through the day, remember what you're working for. The reason I work so hard is so I can leave something for my children.

—Tanya Tucker

Becoming a parent changes everything. You know what's important—that baby. And you know you only get one chance to get it right.

—Garth Brooks

They say you relive your childhood through your kids, and I think that's true. You just have to be careful to let the childhood be your child's and not try to turn it into your own.
— *Alan Jackson*

What seems like a wrong move to some is the perfect move for another. Some people thought my having children without a husband was a big mistake. But how can you look at those two beautiful babies and think they were mistakes?
— *Tanya Tucker*

PATRIOTISM

Patriotism never goes out of style.
   —Lee Greenwood

If we hadn't defended our way of living, our American way of life, in the past—well, there wouldn't be anything to tear up today.
   —Merle Haggard

PERFECTION

Nobody's perfect. The only one who ever was, was crucified.
   —Loretta Lynn

People who are said to be hard to get along with in business are very often just people who want things done right.
   —Tanya Tucker

PERSEVERANCE

You get to a point in a career where you feel like you've been backed up to a cliff, and you've got both the critics and the industry firing bullets at you. You've got two choices—you can either jump and end it all, which is the easy thing to do, or you can stand there and dodge bullets. We dodged the bullets, and they ran out of ammunition.

—Mark Miller
of Sawyer Brown

Hang in there, it'll get better. When old things don't work, try new things. If you bomb horribly, try again. You'll gain confidence.

—Martina McBride

PESSIMISM

I have a lot of energy, and I can direct it either positively or negatively. I've found out that when I direct it negatively, a lot of bad things happen—mostly to me.
— *Willie Nelson*

Y'all don't worry, 'cause it ain't gonna be all right nohow.
— *Hank Williams*

PHILOSOPHY

The secret to life is hitting your golf ball and watching it go out of bounds, and having enough faith that it will hit a tree and come back in. You can't let it bother you if you hit one ball out of bounds.
—Doug Supernaw

Always let love and strength and wisdom be your guide.
—Willie Nelson

My philosophy has always been to shoot straight and make sure you're the one still standing. Then take your loved one's hand and move it on. More than that, no one can ask for. And more than that, no one really needs.

—Willie Nelson

There was a fellow who won a Nobel Prize for something. When they asked him about his philosophy of life, he said, "Well, I'm with Tom T. Hall—faster horses, younger women, older whiskey, and more money." I thought it was kind of neat for a Nobel Prize winner to have that philosophy.

—Tom T. Hall

POVERTY

I was brought up where you squeezed a penny so hard Lincoln blinks. That doesn't make you a better person, it just makes you appreciate it when you make a dollar.
—Vern Gosdin

When you grow up poor, like I did, you have to try and look at the lighter side of it. Not that being poor is all hoots and giggles. But if you look at it the right way, there's bound to have been some funny moments.
—Mark Miller
of Sawyer Brown

THE PRICE OF SUCCESS

You have to pay a price for anything that is worthwhile in life. But I don't think you should ever resent having paid that price. It's so much easier to appreciate what you've got when it doesn't come easy.
—Larry Boone

If you let success change you for the worse, then what you've done is cheat yourself and everybody else.
—Doug Stone

If you become successful at anything, there will always be plenty of people around to take the credit for it.
—Tom T. Hall

PRIDE

Sometimes the things you're proudest of aren't quite real. I remember as a child picking two hundred pounds of cotton one day and feeling pretty proud of myself, until I saw that half of what I'd picked up was leaves.

—Charley Pride

PROBLEMS

I really am basically "The Happiest Girl In The Whole U.S.A." It was more than just a song title for me. I have a wonderful husband, and I've enjoyed a good life. Any other problems can't overshadow those things. That's the key, not letting a little bit of bad hide a whole lot of good.

—Donna Fargo

You don't ever get rid of your problems. You just get a new set.
　　　　　—*Willie Nelson*

So many things have to be right in a relationship these days. Everybody wants a custom fit in an off-the-rack world.
　　　　　—Collin Raye

Women shouldn't be bound by outdated traditions when it comes to picking mates. Older men have been chasing younger girls for years, so it should be okay for women to be involved with younger guys. Why should I go around with some old fuddy-duddy?
　　　　　—*Dottie West*

RESPECT

Success is always temporary. When all is said and done, the only thing you'll have left is your character.
—*Vince Gill*

RISK

What are you going to do, waste your youth? Wait until you're old and then regret never trying? I would rather try everything, and when I'm old, regret a few things I did than regret not doing anything at all.
—Dolly Parton

You can't play it safe forever. My daddy always told me there's only two things in the middle of the road—yellow lines and dead possums.
—Billy Ray Cyrus

I don't believe a person is ever really going to get to do what he wants in life unless he's willing to stick out his neck.
—David Frizzell

ROOTS

It always helps to remember your roots. I remember very well how it is to pick cotton ten hours a day and to plow and cut wood. I remember it so well, I guess, because I don't intend to do it again.
—Johnny Cash

If you wonder why you are the way you are, look at where you came from. I'm a Texas girl. That's where my roots are, and that's probably why I've always done things to excess. We like things larger than life in the Lone Star state.
—*Tanya Tucker*

My dad told me, "Always know where you are and always know where you're going, but don't ever forget where you came from."
— *Billy Ray Cyrus*

My name may be in big lights, but it's still spelled "Country."
— Loretta Lynn

It's good to live where you're originally from, because your roots keep your feet on the ground.
— **Moe Bandy**

If you were raised in Oklahoma, you were raised with all you need.
— *Garth Brooks*

RULES

We did everything back-
wards. We broke every rule
ever written, but we did it.
Don't allow rules to keep
you out of the game.
        —Naomi Judd

SELF-AWARENESS

Always remember your judgment is as good as anybody else's and that being yourself is the easiest thing in the world to do.
—Vern Gosdin

You have to dig down deep to find out who you are. Then, you have to remain true to the person you've found. That's the trick.
—Holly Dunn

Don't worry if you aren't the person you think you ought to be. You spend years working at being a good and whole person. When you're eighteen, you don't know who you are and you don't know what you want to be. I'm twenty-four now, and I'm still trying to figure out what I want to do and be. I just want to be a happy person.
—Shelby Lynn

SELF-RELIANCE

If you're going to live or die by the sword, it better be your own sword, and not somebody else's.
—Travis Tritt

Nobody is going to look after you but you.
—Ray Stevens

I prefer to go in my own direction and let someone follow me.
—Roger Miller

Saying someone is an innovator is just another way of saying they think for themselves.
—Tanya Tucker

SELF-WORTH

Until you understand that
you're worth something, you
can't really give to others.
　　　　　—Tanya Tucker

*Anytime you're having
problems in your life, it
probably has started with
how you feel about yourself.*
　　　　　—Johnny Rodriguez

*In life, you have to get out
there and believe in yourself.*
　　　　　—Naomi Judd

SEX SYMBOLS

It's never too late. I've decided to be a fifty-five-year-old, middle-aged sex symbol.
—Waylon Jennings

I want to be an eighty-year-old lady whose sex life they're still wonderin' about.
—Dolly Parton

SINNERS

We will never stop paying for our sins of the past until we change our thinking about the present.
—Willie Nelson

No one needs a preacher to tell them they're a sinner.
—Waylon Jennings

STARTING OVER

You can't undo what's been done. Once you tear a piece of cloth, it's torn. You can sew it back up, but you might be better off to throw it away and start over with a new piece of cloth.
—Glen Campbell

SUCCESS

Success magnifies everything out of proportion.
—Joe Bonsall
of the Oak Ridge Boys

To really be a success, you've got to be you and nothing else.
—Loretta Lynn

Success is like a bird. If you hold it too tight, you'll kill it. If you don't hold it tight enough, it'll fly away.
—Jimmy Newman

Success? Boy, it's like jumpin' into a car doing eighty.
—Clint Black

Success is that point where the real work begins.
—Terri Gibbs

Any success you have in life belongs to not just you, but to the people who believed in you.
—Mark Chesnutt

Success is not measured by where you are today, but by where you were last year at this time.
—Michelle Wright

It's easy to get that first chance at success—and it's very hard to get a second.
—J.P. Pennington
of Exile

SURVIVING

I feel like an old tree that got shook by the wind and blew over, then sprang back up. I'm a survivor.
—Skeeter Davis
on her longevity in the business

I think we live a lot more off our survival instincts than we dare say. After all, we're really not that many generations removed from the hunter-gatherers.
—*Hal Ketchum*

TAKING A STAND

There are times in life when you have to make a stand if it's something you believe in. But a lot of times, you'd be better off to let things be and they'll probably take care of themselves.
—Ronnie Milsap

You've got to stand for something from being a soldier or not being a soldier, to paying too much rent or not paying too much rent, or fighting a traffic ticket or being the guy that wrote the ticket.
—Aaron Tippin

It's good when people recognize you, but it's better when they recogize that you stand for something.
—Marty Stuart

TESTS

I think everything we go through is a test, and I don't think we're ever asked to endure anything that we can't endure.

— *Willie Nelson*

You have to look at bad things and figure it's just one more test of your determination. All the bad things that have happened to me have been part of a test. It's just waves. Chrisopher Columbus had to sail through a few of them, and look what he discovered.

— Doug Supernaw

TRENDS

You've got people who set trends and people who follow trends. It's not so important which you are, but be sure that the trends you either set or follow are worthwhile.

—Ed Bruce

UNDERSTANDING

One of the things I've learned in life is that when people seem like they're acting a little crazy, you have to ask yourself what their motivations are. Sometimes then they don't seem so crazy.

—Clint Black

VALUES

I think the more simple your values are, the better. I'm kind of simple. I like nice things, but I don't like nice things that don't have any purpose. Like jewelry—I don't wear it because you don't get any use out of it.
—Marty Brown

When you stay true to your heart and your values, you can't go wrong.
—Deborah Allen

Your values will catch up with you. If they are worthwhile and lofty, then you'll find worthwhile things in life. If they are based on greed, you'll probably trip over them.
—Joe Sun

WINNING

Don't play it safe. Always go for the knockout, rather than trying to win on points.
—Collin Raye

Never get into a mind set where losing is what you expect. I've had both wins and losses, and believe me, winning is better.
—Rodney Crowell

WOMANHOOD

Eve was the only woman without a past.
— *Naomi Judd*

Keep your chin up and your skirt down.
— Patsy Cline
her advice to women in country music

I like the line, "You'll never break the woman in me, but you might hurt the child." I think a great many women can relate to that. A lot of women can stand up under a lot of pressure, and they should never forget it.
— *Crystal Gayle*

There're a lot of women out there who need to know they can do it. It's nice to have a man in your life. But—and I want to stress this—we can do it on our own.
—Lorrie Morgan

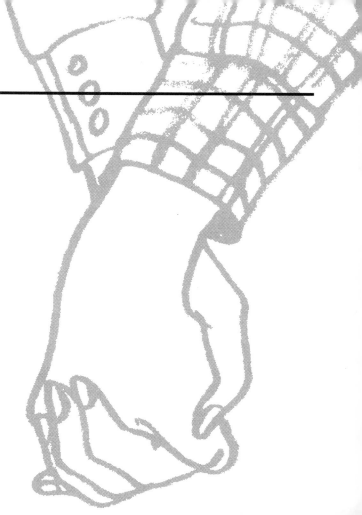

WORK

Somewhere along the way we started to make it a shame to go out and dig a ditch. Well, that's bull-hockey. That's just as important as putting a man on the moon.
—Aaron Tippin

WORRY

Let's not freak out about tomorrow, because it just might not get here.
—Michelle Wright

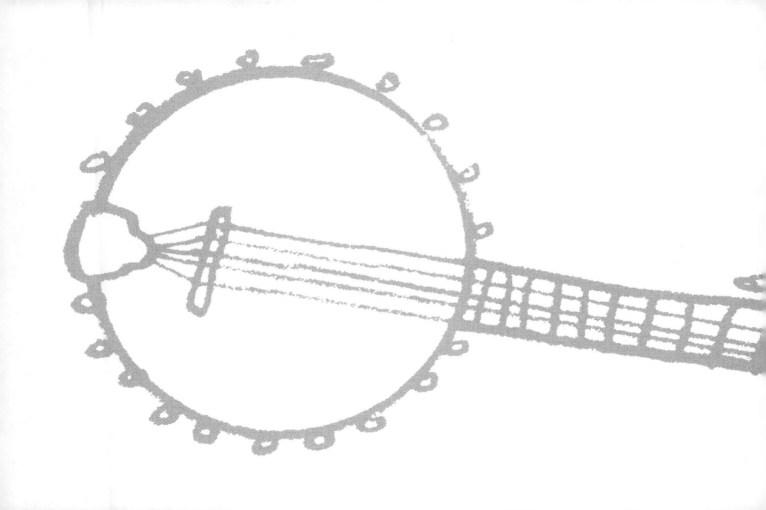

Other Nash & Zullo books available from Andrews and McMeel

Amazing But True Golf Facts
Amazing But True Fishing Stories
The Hollywood Walk of Shame
Amazing But True Cat Tales
Gutter Humor
Amazing But True Dog Tales